THE
SOUTH CENTRAL
STATES

T☆H☆E
SOUTH CENTRAL STATES

HAROLD AND
GERALDINE WOODS

A GROLIER COMPANY

FRANKLIN WATTS
NEW YORK★LONDON★TORONTO★SYDNEY★1984
A FIRST BOOK

Maps by Vantage Art, Inc.

Cover photographs courtesy of:
Oklahoma Tourism,
Texas Highway Department,
Louisiana Office of Tourism,
Shell Oil Company

Photographs courtesy of: New York Public Library
Picture Collection: pp. 8, 11, 17 (top), 21; Woolaroc
Museum: p. 14; Oklahoma University, Western History
Collections: p. 17 (bottom); Fred A. Schell: p. 18;
United Press International: p. 22; Texas Highway
Department: pp. 26, 30; Shell Oil Company: pp. 29,
48; Houston Chamber of Commerce: p. 33; Oklahoma Tourism: pp. 36, 39; Ginger Giles: p. 40; Mississippi River Commission, Corps of Engineers: p. 44;
Louisiana Office of Tourism: pp. 46, 47, 51; Arkansas
Department of Parks and Tourism: p. 54, John
Thomas: p. 55; International Cotton Council: p. 58;
Charles Bickford: p. 60.

Library of Congress Cataloging in Publication Data

Woods, Harold.
The south central states.

(A First book)
Includes index.
Summary: Introduces the history, geography,
agriculture, industry, cities, and sights of
Texas, Oklahoma, Louisiana, and Arkansas.
1. Southwest, Old—Juvenile literature. 2. Oklahoma—
Juvenile literature. [1. Southwest, Old. 2. Oklahoma]
I. Woods, Geraldine. II. Title.
F396.W66   1984   976   83-16868
ISBN 0-531-04737-7

CONTENTS

Chapter One
Geography 1

Chapter Two
History 5

Chapter Three
Texas 24

Chapter Four
Oklahoma 35

Chapter Five
Louisiana 43

Chapter Six
Arkansas 53

Conclusion 62

Index 63

Blytheville

Mississippi River

Jonesboro
West
Memphis

ARKANSAS

Ozark Plateau

BUFFALO RIVER
NATIONAL PARK

Fayetteville

Conway
Little Rock
Monroe

Fort Smith
HOT SPRINGS
NATIONAL PARK
Pine
Bluff
El Dorado

Hot Springs
Arkadelphia
Magnolia

Shreveport

Marshall

Nacogdoches

LOUISIANA

Alexandria

New
Iberia

Baton Rouge
Lake
Pontchartrain

New Orleans

Houma

Mississippi Delta

Lake Charles

Gulf of Mexico

Bartlesville

Muskogee

OKLAHOMA

Oklahoma City

Shawnee

Tulsa

Ponca City

Stillwater

Norman

Ada

Ardmore

Durant

Paris

Texarkana

Longview

Tyler

Corsicana

Lufkin

Huntsville

Beaumont

Baytown

Port Arthur

Galveston

Coastal
Plain

Arkansas R.

Red R.

Guymon

Woodward

Enid

Fairview

Elk City

Altus

Lawton

Wichita Falls

Denison

Sherman

Fort Worth

Dallas

Greenville

Abilene

TEXAS

Waco

Killeen

Temple

Bryan

Houston

Austin

San Marcos

San Antonio

Victoria

Gulf
Coastal
Plain

Corpus Christi

Kingsville

Laredo

Harlingen

Brownsville

McAllen

Borger

Amarillo

Plainview

Lubbock

Big Spring

Midland

Odessa

Pecos

Fort Stockton

San Angelo

Sonora

Uvalde

Crystal City

Del Rio

Rio
Grande

Alpine

BIG BEND
NATIONAL
PARK

El Paso

GUADALUPE MOUNTAINS
NATIONAL PARK

ROCKY MOUNTAINS

★ State Capital

● National Park

• Major City

GEOGRAPHY

R. L. Thornton, an early leader of Dallas, Texas, once said, "Ain't nobody built anything big enough in Dallas. As soon as it's built, it's outgrowed." In a way, Thornton's words could be applied to all four of the south central states: Texas, Oklahoma, Louisiana, and Arkansas. They are part of the Sun Belt, which is one of the fastest-growing regions in the United States. In the 1980s, these states have more people, more houses, and more industry than ever before.

Yet only a few decades ago, the Sun Belt states had another name: the Deep South. This term brought to mind the image of a poor, mostly agricultural area that was slow to change and plagued with bitter racial tensions.

How did the Deep South become the Sun Belt? There were many reasons for the change. One of those reasons was the land itself. Ages ago, much of the south central United States was under water. In those ancient seas, fish swam and plants grew. After death, the animals and vegetables sank to the sea floor, where they were covered by many layers of sand and dirt. These remains of ancient plants and animals were subject to tremendous pressures within the earth. Gradually, they were transformed into oil and coal, riches which today are attracting people, business, and industry.

The sea that covered the south central states has long since dried up. Much of the area is now part of the Gulf Coastal Plain, a low, mostly flat area bordering the Gulf of Mexico. The eastern half of Texas, all of Louisiana, and the southeastern portions of Arkansas and Oklahoma are located on the Gulf Coastal Plain. Inland, the Plain is hilly and often covered with forests. In many places, deer, cougars, raccoons, and an occasional bear are found. Near the sea are beaches and fresh- or saltwater marshes and swamps. In Louisiana, the coast winds in and out, forming many bays and inlets. Slow-moving streams called bayous thread through the swamps. Cypress trees, often hung with a stringy gray plant called Spanish moss, grow near the bayous. There is a variety of animal life, including alligators.

The Coastal Plain is warm and humid. Winds from the Gulf keep winters mild and prevent summer temperatures from rising too high. The average temperature in January is only about 50°F (10°C), rising to an average of 82°F (28°C) in July. Thunderstorms are common in this region, as are tornadoes, and hurricanes often buffet the coast. These hurricanes can be very dangerous. In 1969, Hurricane Camille destroyed 5,000 homes.

In northeastern Oklahoma and northwestern Arkansas, the land rises to a high plateau. Through the centuries, streams and rivers cut into the land, and wind and rain wore it away. Today, the Ozark Plateau, as the region is called, is filled with rolling hills and deep valleys. There are so many hills that some people call the area the Ozark Mountains. The land is thickly forested with oak and hickory trees and rich in wildlife such as deer and bear. The weather is cooler and less humid than the coastal area. Summer days are hot, averaging about 80°F (27°C). There are occasional light snowfalls in winter, when the temperature falls to an average of 42°F (6°C). South of the Ozark Plateau and the Boston Mountains are the tree-covered Ouachita Mountains, known for their hot springs.

Most of Oklahoma is flat, grassy land, part of the Central and Great Plains. The Great Plains also extend into western and southern Texas. When the first settlers came to these Plains, enormous herds of buffalo grazed there. Now, buffalo live only in wildlife preserves. However, coyotes, jackrabbits, and other animals can still be found.

Winter weather on the Plains can be bitter, though summers are warm. West Texas is occasionally swept by fierce storms called "Blue Northers." There is enough rainfall in the eastern portion of the Plains, though in the west rainfall averages only 12 to 16 inches (30.5 to 40.6 cm) a year, and droughts are fairly common.

The North Central Plains, located in northern Texas, are also flat; the deep, rich soil of this area is very fertile. In southwestern Texas are the Mexican Highlands, which are crossed by extensions of the Rocky Mountains. Most of these hilly regions of Texas are home to a curious animal called the armadillo. Armadillos are covered with bony plates that look like miniature suits of armor.

THE MIGHTY RIVER

Threading through the plains of the south central states is America's most important river, the Mississippi. The Mississippi begins as a small stream near the northern border of the United States. As it passes through America's heartland, 250 other rivers flow into it. The Mississippi gains strength and becomes a water highway. Pleasure boats, freighters, huge barges, and tankers travel upon it.

All the facts about the Mississippi seem larger than life. It is over 2,300 miles (3,700 km) long, drains thirty-one states, and carries 40,000,000 tons (36,000,000 mt) of freight each year. Each day it dumps enough soil at its mouth on the Gulf of Mexico to fill a freight train 150 miles (241 km) long. Through the centuries, this soil has filled in parts of the Gulf, creating a wedge of land called the Mississippi Delta. The Delta, which covers 15,000 square miles (38,850 sq km) of Louisiana, is still growing at the rate of 1,000 acres (405 ha) a year.

The mighty Mississippi is also a wild river. At times it changes course, sometimes carving new channels almost overnight. Often, the river overflows its banks, flooding the surrounding countryside. To control flooding, pumping stations are located along the river. In many places, sheets of steel mesh and levees (mounds of earth) line the banks to keep the shore from washing away. In spite of all this, the Mississippi still floods from time to time. In December 1982, the river destroyed huge areas of farmland and many homes in Arkansas and Louisiana. Two hundred people were injured and 10,000 were left homeless.

The Mississippi's floods have deposited a thick layer of rich soil on the surrounding land, and so have those of other rivers in the south central states, such as the Rio Grande, Arkansas, and Red rivers. Consequently, these rivers have created some of the best farmland in the United States.

☆2☆

HISTORY

As early as 25,000 years ago, human beings were living in the south central states. Scientists have found the remains of many prehistoric societies. Some are "only" 1,500 years old; others are more ancient. Pottery, baskets, arrowheads, and other remains of these peoples may be seen in museums today.

Gradually, those prehistoric peoples formed tribes and developed their own languages, art, and life-styles. In Louisiana one of the largest tribes was the Caddo. They lived in huts thatched with palmetto leaves and plastered with clay. They grew corn, melons, beans, and tobacco, and sailed in hollowed-out logs called pirogues. The Caddo also lived in Arkansas and Texas. Other Arkansan Indians include the Quapaw and Osage tribes. The Quapaw's and Osage's homeland extended into Oklahoma, where they lived in permanent villages and farmed the land. The Apache, Cheyenne, and other tribes of western Oklahoma and Texas moved constantly from place to place, hunting buffalo for food. Other Texan tribes were the Tonkawas, who lived in the center of the state, and the Karankawas and Attacapas, from the coastal areas.

THE EUROPEANS
ARRIVE

In 1528, the Karankawas captured a shipwrecked Spaniard, Cabeza de Vaca, who had washed ashore on Galveston Island, Texas. De Vaca was one of the first European explorers in search of riches and new colonies for Europe to reach the south central states. The Spaniard escaped seven years later and traveled on foot through Texas and the Southwest until he reached California. De Vaca's countryman, Francisco Coronado, led a band of explorers through Texas and Oklahoma in 1541. Coronado was searching for a legendary city made of gold and jewels. As he traveled, he left some horses and cattle behind. The animals multiplied and were soon adopted by the Indians of western Oklahoma, who became excellent riders.

Around the same time, a nineteen-year-old boy named Hernando de Soto sailed to Central America to seek fame and fortune. After spending time in Peru and Cuba, de Soto traveled to North America and began to explore. In 1541, he found the Mississippi, which he named El Rio del Espiritu Santo ("The River of the Holy Spirit").

In 1673, two Frenchmen, Father Jacques Marquette and Louis Joliet, sailed down the Mississippi as far as the Arkansas River. Nine years later another Frenchman, Robert René Cavelier La Salle, completed the trip to the mouth of the Mississippi.

La Salle claimed all the land drained by the Mississippi for France. He was following the custom of the day; explorers usually felt that their kings were entitled to all the land they traveled through. La Salle knew that there were Indians living in the Mississippi Valley, but he was not concerned about them. To La Salle, and to most Europeans at that time, the Indians were savages. They had no more right to the land than the deer or the buffalo that grazed on it.

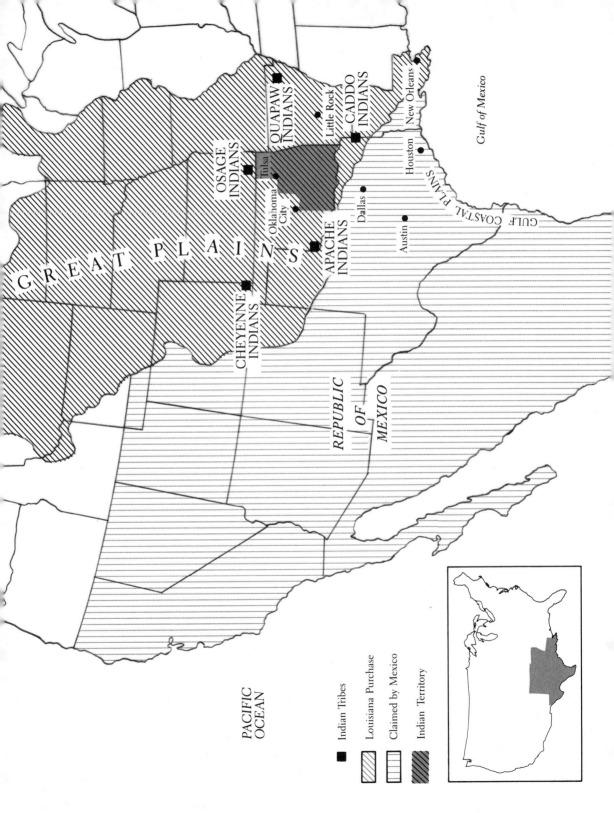

QUAPAW INDIANS

CADDO INDIANS

Little Rock

New Orleans

Gulf of Mexico

OSAGE INDIANS

Tulsa

Houston

Oklahoma City

Dallas

APACHE INDIANS

Austin

GULF COASTAL PLAINS

G R E A T   P L A I N S

CHEYENNE INDIANS

REPUBLIC OF MEXICO

PACIFIC OCEAN

Indian Tribes

Louisiana Purchase

Claimed by Mexico

Indian Territory

The Indians, of course, felt differently. In the early years of exploration and colonization, when European settlements were small and widely spaced, many Indians were willing to share the land. However, as more and more settlers arrived, the Indians often fought for their homelands. They lost most battles because of the Europeans' superior weapons.

During the 1600s and 1700s, new settlements sprang up throughout the south central states. The Spanish established missions in Texas. Henri de Tonti built a trading post on the Arkansas River called Arkansas Post. A French-Canadian named Jean Baptiste Le Wayne Bienville founded New Orleans in 1718.

In 1754, the European nations fought the French and Indian War to settle their claims in the New World. In 1763, Britain defeated France and Spain, and won vast areas of eastern North America. Spain controlled the south central area. In 1800, Spain gave the Louisiana Territory, including the present states of Louisiana, Arkansas, and Oklahoma, to France.

THE LOUISIANA PURCHASE

In 1803, the United States was a struggling young country extending from the Atlantic Ocean to the Mississippi River, from the southern border of Canada to the northern border of Florida. President Thomas Jefferson knew that control of the Mississippi, and especially the port of New Orleans, was important to the nation's

Troops fire a 21-gun salute as the Stars and Stripes are raised in this painting of the celebration of the Louisiana Purchase in 1803.

—9—

survival. The settlers in the upper Mississippi Valley needed the river to transport their goods to the Gulf of Mexico, where they could be loaded on larger ships and taken to Europe, the Indies, or South America. Jefferson sent representatives to France to try to buy New Orleans or a small strip of land west of the river. If France would not sell, the Americans were to arrange a treaty giving the United States the right to travel on the Mississippi.

However, Napoleon Bonaparte, the ruler of France, had another deal in mind. His government was desperately in need of money. Also, Britain, still an enemy of France, clearly wanted to capture New Orleans. So Napoleon made a shocking offer. The United States could buy 800,000 square miles (2,072,000 sq km) of land—for only four cents an acre! The total price was $15,000,000, and it was all or nothing; Napoleon was not interested in a smaller sale.

Jefferson quickly agreed to this amazing bargain. The Louisiana Purchase, as the deal came to be called, *doubled* the territory of the United States. Incredibly, some Americans opposed the purchase. Many thought it was too expensive; others said the huge territory would never be fit for civilization!

Settlers soon flocked to the area. In 1812, the southern section of the territory became the state of Louisiana. Arkansas, another part of the Louisiana Purchase, was admitted to the Union in 1836.

REMEMBER THE ALAMO!

The cost of land in Texas was also low, though the price was paid by American settlers instead of by the United States government. Spain had originally occupied Texas, as well as Mexico and other land in North and South America. When Mexico won its independence from Spain in 1821, Texas became part of the new Republic of Mexico.

The desperate courage of Davy Crockett and
the 186 other Americans who died defending
their fort is shown in Robert Onderdonk's
painting, "Fall of the Alamo."

Texas at that time was inhabited by few people. To encourage settlement, in 1824 the Mexican government offered American families 4,428 acres (1,792 ha) of land each, tax-free for ten years. In return the colonists had to pay $30, take an oath of allegiance to Mexico, and promise to follow the Catholic religion. It was an attractive offer, and settlers came from as far away as New England to take advantage of it. Some spent months in preparation; others simply wrote "GTT" ("Gone To Texas") on their cabin doors and left.

By 1830, 75 percent of the people in Texas were Americans, and the Mexican government began to lose control of the province. Many colonists refused to practice the required religion; some kept slaves (which were illegal in Mexico) and disobeyed trade rules.

Too late, the Mexican government decided to tighten its control over Texas. It stopped selling land to Americans, passed new laws regulating slavery and trade, and required all foreigners to have passports. In 1831, Mexican troops were sent to enforce the law. The colonists reacted angrily. They had become accustomed to their own way of life. Now it seemed as if the Mexican government was trying to take away their freedom.

In 1835, war broke out. A year later, 187 Americans tried to defend their fort, the Alamo, against an army of 3,000 Mexicans. They were hopelessly outnumbered. During the struggle all the Americans, including such famous men as Davy Crockett, Jim Bowie, and Colonel William Travis, were killed. Their courage inspired other Texans. Cries of "Remember the Alamo!" were heard in every battle. A month after the Alamo, the Mexican army was defeated at the Battle of San Jacinto, and the Republic of Texas was established.

Nine years later, Texas asked Congress for permission to join the United States. On December 29, 1845, Texas became the twenty-eighth state.

THE INDIAN TERRITORY

While Texans were fighting for independence from Mexico, the residents of the area we now call Oklahoma were trying to create a new way of life for themselves. These early Oklahomans were members of the Cherokee, Chickasaw, Choctaw, Seminole, and Creek tribes. They were called the "Five Civilized Tribes" by the United States government. The Five Civilized Tribes had originally lived in the southeastern United States, on land desired by American settlers. By treaty and at times by force, the government had moved the Five Civilized Tribes westward to a section of the Louisiana Purchase. The government divided the new "Indian Territory" into five areas, one for each of the tribes.

The tribes' various trips to the Indian Territory has been called the "Trail of Tears." The Indians often traveled in bad weather, without enough food. About one-third of each tribe died along the way. When they arrived in the Indian Territory, the Five Civilized Tribes quickly wrote constitutions, elected officials, and built schools, hospitals, post offices, and courts. There was nothing primitive about their way of life. The Choctaws, for example, were ruled by a chief, three lesser chiefs, and a tribal council. Later the Choctaws established a senate and a house of representatives. The Cherokees printed the Territory's first newspaper, *The Cherokee Advocate*. The stories were written in both English and Cherokee. The Cherokees also built many government buildings that are still in use today. Though they had a shaky beginning, the Indians believed they now had a secure homeland. Their land had been promised to them for "as long as the grass grows and the waters run."

THE CIVIL WAR

Unfortunately, civil war soon swept through the United States. For years, the North and the South had disagreed on many issues,

especially slavery, which was legal in the South and outlawed in the North.

In the south central states, many people believed the only solution was to break away from the United States to form a separate country. Not everyone agreed. In western Arkansas and western Texas, where there were few slaves, most people wanted to stay in the Union. However, in 1861, war broke out. Texas, Louisiana, and other southern states formed the Confederate States of America. Arkansas was divided. Its government voted to join the Confederacy, but a rival Union government was soon set up. The Indian Territory was also split; many small "civil wars" were fought between Confederate and Union supporters.

When the South was finally defeated in 1865, its economy was nearly destroyed. Trade and industry had suffered during the war, and the farming system had collapsed. Before the war, most of the South's huge farms, or plantations, had depended on slave labor. After the war the slaves were freed, and the plantation system was in ruins. The South was also placed under Union military rule for a few years after the war. The Northern officials often managed state affairs for their own profit, instead of for the good of the people.

All of this added up to poverty for the south central states. Louisiana, which was one of the richest states in 1860, went bankrupt in 1874. Texas and Arkansas also had financial problems. In some ways the Indian Territory suffered most of all. The Five Civilized Tribes were punished because some of their members

Uprooted from their home-
lands by American settlers,
Indians were forced to
travel the "Trail of Tears."

had supported the Confederacy. The U.S. government took away some of their land and gave it to several tribes who were moved into the Territory from other areas.

LAND RUSH

The Pawnee, Apache, Comanche, and other tribes who arrived in the Indian Territory after the Civil War also believed that the land was theirs forever. However, once again American settlements were expanding. "Boomers"—homesteaders in covered wagons—began to arrive at the borders of the Indian Territory. There they made camp and tried to persuade the government to open the Indians' land to settlers.

In 1889 they succeeded. A small piece of land in the center of the Indian Territory was made available. It was soon settled in a most amazing way. On the morning of April 22, boomers lined up along the borders of the Territory. Exactly at noon, soldiers shot their rifles into the air. The race was on! On horseback, in covered wagons, and on foot, people raced to claim a piece of land. In a matter of hours, all the lots were taken.

Above: *wagons stream into the Indian Territory in Oklahoma during the 1889 land rush. Below: for the early settlers, schooling was often makeshift. Here, classes are held in a tree branch "schoolhouse" in Live Oak County, Texas, in the late 1880s.*

Boiler A
Apri[l]

During the next ten years, many more races were held. Each time, the Indians were allowed to keep small pieces of land for their own families. The extra land, which had been owned by the tribe as a whole, was purchased by the government and opened to settlement. Soon, the entire Indian Territory was dotted with farms and cities. In 1907, Oklahoma became the forty-sixth state.

OIL!

At the turn of the century, a man named Pattillo Higgins studied the land near Beaumont in West Texas. He predicted that oil would be found in an area called Spindletop. Experts laughed at Higgins' ideas, and offered to drink all the oil he found. Luckily, Higgins never held them to their promise. On January 10, 1901, drillers struck oil. The first well produced as much oil in one year as all the other 37,000 wells in the eastern United States. In the next few years, oil was discovered at many other sites in Texas, Oklahoma, and Louisiana. Later, a small amount of the valuable mineral was found in Arkansas.

Wherever there was a large quantity of oil, the economy boomed, and many people became wealthy. However, the oil wealth was not shared by everyone in the south central states. A large number of people, particularly those who worked on small farms, were barely able to make a living.

The Spindletop oil strike was soon depleted by the forest of derricks that sprang up there.

In 1929, the Great Depression began, and the American economy nearly collapsed. Businesses went bankrupt, banks failed, and unemployment rose to record levels. Farmers were especially hard hit. A drought had dried up farmland and windstorms had blown the topsoil away. The once fertile plain became known as the "Dust Bowl." As the farm economy collapsed, poverty-stricken "Arkies" from Arkansas and "Okies" from Oklahoma left their states and traveled west, hoping to find work.

President Franklin D. Roosevelt's New Deal and the coming of World War II ended the Depression, and the south central states began to recover. New irrigation projects and improved methods of farming prevented the fields from becoming another Dust Bowl. Many military bases were created or expanded, and new industries based on oil and its by-products were established. This provided more jobs and increased the states' income.

THE STRUGGLE FOR EQUALITY

With the end of the Civil War, slavery was outlawed. All Americans—black and white—were declared equal. Unfortunately, real equality could not come from a simple declaration. Racist attitudes, inherted from the days of master and slave, proved hard to change. After the war, many Southern towns passed laws aimed at keeping blacks and whites separate. Although blacks were guaranteed the right to vote by the Constitution, many were prevented from using that right. Also, blacks were often forced into second-class schools and jobs. This created a pattern of high unemployment and poverty among black people.

A desolate Oklahoma
Dust Bowl farm in 1936

In the 1950s and 1960s, blacks began to press for their civil rights. Some of the most intense struggles took place in the south central states. In Little Rock, Arkansas, for example, blacks and whites had been required to attend separate high schools. In 1954, the Supreme Court said that such separation was illegal. Three years later, the first black students entered Central High School in Little Rock. A crowd of angry white people gathered outside. Federal troops had to protect the black students as they entered the building.

Conflicts like this took place throughout the south central states for many years. However, progress has been made and racial attitudes have begun to change.

During the court-ordered desegregation of Central High School in Little Rock, Arkansas, black students were escorted into the school by the National Guard.

☆3☆

TEXAS

In 1883, Texan officials were considering plans for a new capitol building for their state. They admired the dome of the nation's capitol in Washington, D.C. However, a dome like that is very expensive. So the legislature came up with an idea: Texas would pay the builder with land instead of money. The offer was accepted and everyone was pleased. Texas got a new capitol; in return the construction company got 3,000,000 acres (1,214,100 ha) of land, which became the XIT Ranch.

The XIT Ranch is a good example of why most people think big when they think of Texas. The state itself was the largest in the Union for a long time, with 267,338 square miles (692,405 sq km) of land. When Alaska became a state, Texas dropped to second place.

Texans have always enjoyed joking about size. They like to tell visitors about grapefruits as big as houses, roaches so large their shadows weigh 10 pounds (4.5 kg) and other tall tales. Outsiders have also made jokes about the Lone Star State (Texas gets that name from its flag, which has one star). One cartoon shows a Texan cowboy resting on a pile of dollar bills as an oil well pumps busily. Though of course it is an exaggeration, this cartoon does contain a bit of truth. A few Texans did become fabulously wealthy from oil and natural gas deposits in their state. However, most did not.

To most people, Texas also means cowboys. Cowboys have been linked with the state since Spanish settlers brought cattle to graze on Texan grasslands. The early cowboys cared for the animals throughout their lives, branding young calves and rounding up the mature animals for market. Today, Texan cowboys (and cowgirls) perform the same chores—with a few changes. Modern cowboys give their cattle the latest medicines, vaccinate them against disease, and distribute feed in winter. Very often, today's "cowpokes" *drive* their horses to work in trailers, before saddling up for the day. In spite of these differences, Texans still value their cowboy traditions. Rodeos are popular entertainments in Texas; when one important show arrives for a yearly performance in Houston, schoolchildren are given a holiday!

However, only a few Texans are cowboys and -girls. Other Texans are farmers, factory workers, computer designers, and even astronauts. Many space flights have communicated with earth through NASA's Mission Control in Houston.

"TEX-MEX"

According to the 1980 census, there are over 14,000,000 Texans, including 1,700,000 blacks and almost 3,000,000 Hispanic citizens. The Lone Star State reflects its strong Mexican and Spanish heritage. "Tex-Mex" cooking is popular; specialties like chili, tacos, and tamales are served in restaurants all over the state. Many homes are built in the Spanish style, with adobe (dried-clay brick) walls. In some parts of Texas, it is possible to speak Spanish at home and on the job, using English only for special occasions.

At times, Mexican-Americans and other minority groups have been victims of prejudice. They have often had a lower stan-

A modern-day cattle roundup
near Marathon, Texas

dard of living and a higher rate of unemployment than other Texans. However, this is changing. In 1981, San Antonio elected a Mexican-American mayor, Henry Cisneros, the first mayor of Hispanic descent in the United States.

Another large group in Texas are illegal aliens—Mexicans who crossed the border secretly in search of better job opportunities. Because they are in the United States illegally, these Mexicans are not protected by law. Many work for extremely low salaries, without medical insurance, pensions, and other benefits. Illegal aliens are also a problem for the state, since they pay no taxes. In 1977, Texas announced that the children of illegal aliens would have to pay tuition if they attended public schools. However, the Supreme Court ruled that this was unconstitutional, and the children now attend for free.

AGRICULTURE AND INDUSTRY

The huge XIT property has been broken up now, but Texas still has some enormous ranches. The King Ranch, for example, contains 1,250,000 acres (505,875 ha). Cattle are raised there and on many smaller ranches throughout Texas. In fact, there are more cattle in Texas than in any other state. Texas also raises more sheep than any other state, and produces the most wool. The rich grass of central Texas feeds large herds of angora goats, who supply almost all the mohair produced in the United States. The Lone Star State also ranks first in shrimp production, and Texan fishermen market many other fish from the Gulf of Mexico.

Cotton, which is grown mainly on the Gulf Coast and on the northern and central plains, is another important agricultural product. Texas grows about a billion pounds (453,600,000 kg) a year, ranking first in the United States. Texas is second in the production of sorghum, a grain that is used to feed animals. Texan farms also grow rice, wheat, corn, oats, soybeans, vegetables, and other crops.

Texas' huge deposits of oil and natural gas make the state the leader in American mining. Sulphur, salt, graphite, magnesium, and other minerals are also produced in Texas. The Lone Star State also supplies equipment for oil production in other countries.

Manufacturing is another important source of income. Chemicals and other products made from oil; machinery; and food products are the leading industries. Metal, plastic, and glass products, clothing, instruments, and wood and paper goods are also made in Texas.

AN ECONOMIC BOOM

A mild climate and plentiful supplies of oil and gas have resulted in cheap energy bills for both factories and homes in the Lone Star State. Consequently, many new industries have been drawn to Texas. Another attraction is the Texan labor force. Traditionally, wages have been lower in the South than in other areas, perhaps because few workers belong to unions.

Industrial growth has brought an economic boom in Texas. In the late 1970s, 100,000 new jobs were created in Dallas, Fort Worth, and Houston. Naturally, such growth lowered the unemployment rate, even during periods when other states experienced a recession (economic hard times). In December 1981, for example, only 4.5 percent of the work force was unemployed in Texas, compared with over 10 percent in some other states.

Because of the low unemployment rate, thousands of workers from other states have flocked to Texas in search of work. Especially in the early years of the economic boom, many found good jobs and settled happily into Texan life. However, recently the Texas economy has started to slow down. In the early 1980s, high-

*The oil industry is critical to
the Texas economy. Shown here is
Shell Oil's Deer Park refinery.*

er costs, lower prices, and smaller demand troubled the oil companies. Some had to lay off workers. Other industries earned lower profits as well, and even farming was affected. For example, the price of cotton fell by 50 percent between 1980 and 1981. All of this has had an effect on the Texas job market. The unemployment rate climbed to 8.8 percent in early 1983. Late that year, the Texas state government printed a pamphlet and distributed it in several other states. The message: if you come to Texas, you may not find a job.

GROWING—
IN MORE WAYS THAN ONE

Rapid growth has brought some problems to Texas. In Houston, for example, most people drive to work. Growth has meant more cars—and more traffic jams. A traffic reporter in Houston remarked that the rush hour in 1975 used to last about an hour and a half. By 1983, the roads were bumper to bumper for a full three hours. Houston is now considering a rail transit system to unclog its streets.

Economic growth has also resulted in more crime. Between 1977 and 1982, reported crime increased 22 percent in Dallas and 30 percent in Austin. Several other Texas cities also experienced higher crime rates.

Ecology is another concern. As more oil wells are drilled in the Gulf of Mexico, there is a greater chance of spills or "blowouts." Spilled oil can spoil beaches and poison birds, fish, and other wildlife. In West Texas, environmentalists are worried about

*Houston is one of the
nation's fastest growing cities.*

water conservation. The area's water comes from wells drilled into a huge natural underground reservoir called the Ogallala Formation. In 1945, there were only 3,500 wells drawing water from the Ogallala. Now there are over 200,000 wells. There is danger that the water will simply be exhausted someday.

CITIES AND SIGHTS

Austin, the state capital, was founded a few years after Texas became independent from Mexico. From the beginning, Austin was planned as a dignified, stately city—an appropriate setting for the new Texan government. Besides the domed capitol and other government buildings, Austin is the site of the Lyndon B. Johnson Library. More than 30,000,000 of the former president's papers are housed there.

Houston is the largest city in Texas. Some experts think it will be the largest city in the country by the year 2000. In its early years, Houston was the center of the cattle industry. After oil was discovered, most major American oil companies established offices there. Although it is 51 miles (82 km) from the coast, Houston is connected to the Gulf of Mexico by the Houston Ship Channel, a man-made canal. Houston is one of the busiest ports in the United States, handling cotton, oil, and other products. Houston has one of the tallest monuments in the world, a memorial to the Battle of San Jacinto. Another huge building is the Astrodome, the headquarters of the Houston Astros baseball and the Oilers football teams.

The man-made Houston Ship Channel, connecting Houston with the Gulf of Mexico, has made Houston one of the busiest ports in the world.

In 1841, Dallas' first settler, John Neely Bryan, named a city "for my friend Dallas," George Dallas, then vice-president of the United States. Today, Dallas is a leading banking and insurance center, and the headquarters of a growing aerospace and computer industry. Important sights in Dallas include Fair Park, where the Texas State Fair is held, the Museum of Fine Arts, and a memorial to President John F. Kennedy, who was assassinated while visiting the city.

Year admitted to Union: 1845
Capital: Austin
Nickname: Lone Star State
Motto: "Friendship"
Flower: bluebonnet
Bird: mockingbird
Song: "Texas, Our Texas"
Flag: a vertical blue stripe with a
       single star and two horizontal
       stripes (red and white).

☆ **4** ☆

OKLAHOMA

On the morning of April 22, 1889, it was just a flat prairie. By evening, only hours after the Land Rush ended, it was a city— Oklahoma City, with 10,000 people, some tents, and not much else.

Today, 400,000 people live in Oklahoma City. There are over 3,000,000 residents in the entire Sooner State. (Oklahoma gets its nickname from the homesteaders who sneaked into the Indian Territory "sooner" than they should have.) Many Oklahomans are descendents of the original settlers. A large number are Indians. In fact, one-third of all the Indians in the United States live in Oklahoma. Unlike tribes in other states, most of Oklahoma's Indians do not live on reservations. In 1907, their tribal governments were broken up and all the Indians became citizens of the United States.

Most of Oklahoma's Indians have adjusted to modern American life, mingling freely with whites and taking an active role in government and industry. Indians and whites have often intermarried. This Indian heritage is not a source of prejudice in Oklahoma. In fact, it is a source of great pride. Many Oklahomans boast that they are part or pure Indian. Two of the state's governors, one

United States senator, and many other politicians in the Sooner State have been Indians.

However, the change from an Indian to a white culture has not been easy for everyone. In a few areas the Indians are poverty-stricken, with an unemployment rate as high as 40 percent.

Today, Oklahomans show their appreciation of their Indian heritage in a variety of ways. Reconstructed Indian houses are exhibited in Indian City, in southwest Oklahoma. Many cities and towns, such as Tulsa, Muskogee, and Ponca City, have Indian names. Rodeos and Indian dance festivals are popular entertainments.

Oklahoma also has a large black population, numbering about 200,000. There has been much less racial tension in Oklahoma than in other areas of the south central United States. Oklahomans come from many different backgrounds, and they tend to accept differences in races and nationalities fairly easily.

AGRICULTURE AND INDUSTRY

The broad plains of Oklahoma, where huge herds of buffalo used to graze, now provide grass for cattle. Oklahoma has more beef cattle than any other state in the United States except Texas. Pigs, chickens, and sheep are also raised in the Sooner State. Oklahoma's yearly income from livestock is over $500,000,000.

In the 1930s, Oklahoma was the "Dust Bowl." Today, it is a rich agricultural center. Instead of endless straight rows of a single crop, Oklahoma's farms now grow a variety of plants. The change from one crop to another allows the soil to rest and remain fertile.

Indian dance festivals are one of the ways that Oklahomans commemorate their Indian heritage.

Crops are also planted in strips, and plowing follows the curve of the land. This helps prevent topsoil from blowing away. Six large reservoirs have been built in Oklahoma since 1940. Farmers use that water to irrigate the land when there is not enough natural rainfall.

The most important crop grown in Oklahoma is winter wheat, which is raised in the northern and western areas of the state. Cotton is a principal crop in southwestern Oklahoma. Hay, corn, peanuts, and barley are also grown in the Sooner State. More pecans and mung beans are harvested in Oklahoma than in any other state.

The production of oil and natural gas is the largest industry in Oklahoma. The state ranks fourth in the United States in the amount of oil mined each year. There are 5,000 oil wells in the area around Oklahoma City. There is even a well on the grounds of the state capitol!

Oil is a very important part of Oklahoman life. Newspapers devote whole sections to lists of new wells drilled, amounts produced, and other related information. Thousands of people are employed in oil equipment or research firms. Oklahoma also has a good supply of other minerals such as sulfur, lead, and zinc, and has enough coal to supply all of the country's needs for 300 years.

Many of the crops grown in Oklahoma are the raw material for the food processing industry, which brings over $150,000,000 a year to the state. Other important industries are the manufacture of machinery and stone, clay, and glass products. The state's

Oil abounds in Oklahoma and, appropriately, there is even an oil well on the capitol grounds in Oklahoma City.

10,000,000 acres (4,047,000 ha) of forests also supply timber for wood and paper goods produced in Oklahoma.

A good supply of energy as well as a wide variety of industries has helped Oklahoma resist the recessions of the late 1970s and early 1980s. Like Texas, Oklahoma's unemployment rate remained low and its profits high even while the country as a whole was having economic difficulties. In 1981, for example, the unemployment rate in Oklahoma was only 3.6 percent. However, the state has not escaped the economic slump completely. In late 1982, the unemployment rate climbed to 6.3 percent.

Conservation is an important concern in Oklahoma. The state has been careful to prevent industry from spoiling the natural beauty of the land. As one businessman said, the state is interested in payrolls but not pollution. Oklahoma has an active Wildlife Council dedicated to saving the state's animals and has set aside 400,000 acres (161,880 ha) of land as nature preserves.

CITIES AND SIGHTS

Oklahoma City used to be known as a "cow town," having been a hub of the cattle industry since 1910. However, the growth of the oil industry has changed the city's image. Oklahoma City is still a center for meat-packing, but now the energy, food processing, and construction industries are also important. The capital of the state, Oklahoma City, contains many government buildings. Tourists

Although long outranked by the oil industry, cattle-raising is still important in Oklahoma. Here, cattle are being judged at the State Fair in Oklahoma City.

enjoy visiting the National Cowboy Hall of Fame and the State Historical Museum, which has the world's largest collection of Indian relics.

Tulsa, a small village at the turn of the century, is now a modern metropolis of 360,000 people. Tulsa is often called "the oil capital of the world" and is headquarters for 800 oil companies. A man-made waterway connects Tulsa with the Mississippi River; farm products from the Midwest are shipped from Tulsa to the Mississippi and on to the Gulf of Mexico. Tulsa was rated one of the country's "most livable" cities in a recent poll. The city has a modern performing arts center, a ballet, a symphony orchestra, and Oklahoma's only opera company.

Year admitted to Union: 1907
Capital: Oklahoma City
Nickname: Sooner State
Motto: *Labor Omnia Vincit"*
    ("Labor Conquers All Things")
Flower: mistletoe
Bird: scissor-tailed flycatcher
Song: "Oklahoma"
Flag: blue with Osage cowhide shield,
    eagle feathers, olive branch,
    and peace pipe.

☆**5**☆

LOUISIANA

In 1717, a man named John Law printed a series of giant posters and sent them all over Europe. The posters showed a sailing ship anchored in a calm harbor, tall mountains dotted with pleasant wooden houses, and adoring Indians offering gold to well-dressed Europeans. John Law said the picture represented life in Louisiana. He hoped the Europeans who saw the poster would want to settle in the New World.

A few years later, hundreds of Law's colonists arrived in New Orleans. They found marshy land and a few log houses rotting in the damp climate. Not a single mountain was in sight, nor was there any gold. Realizing they had been tricked, all but sixty-eight of the settlers fled in search of better land.

If John Law were to visit Louisiana today, he probably wouldn't believe his eyes. After a shaky beginning, New Orleans has grown into one of the greatest cities in the world. The former swamps are covered with graceful houses and modern skyscrapers. There still aren't any mountains. (New Orleans' highest point is an artificial hill as tall as a one-story house!) However, the harbor is now filled with ships from all over the world. And Law's "gold" turned out to be "black gold"—oil.

The state of Louisiana has also grown. Louisiana now has over 4,000,000 people. About 69 percent are white. Many are of Italian, German, or English ancestry. A large number are Creoles—descendents of the Spanish and French settlers of colonial days. (The term is also applied to people of mixed European and black descent.) Creole culture has been influenced by both Spain and France, as well as by black and Indian traditions. The Creoles are famous for their Mardi Gras, a celebration that involves almost the entire city of New Orleans. "Mardi Gras" means "fat Tuesday" and refers to the day before the Christian season of Lent begins. However, the celebration really starts weeks before. As many as 200 parades and balls are held, with participants dressed in fancy costumes and masks. New Orleanians spend months preparing for the event. Some schools even hold classes on mask-making for children!

Another important group is the Cajuns—descendents of French Canadians who arrived in Louisiana in the 1760s. There are about 500,000 Cajuns in the state today. Many live in rural areas, farming or hunting and fishing along the bayous. Cajuns speak a variety of French that is similar to the language used in Canada 200 years ago. For a long time, Cajun children were forbidden to speak their own language in school. Now French has been recognized as part of the Cajun heritage, and the children are encouraged to learn both French and English.

Cajuns have extremely strong family ties. Relatives often live near each other, relaxing together at a *boucherie* (a type of barbecue) or a *fais dodo*. The words "*fais dodo*" mean "to sleep" and "a dance." Cajun families attend a *fais dodo* together. When they are tired, the children sleep—while their parents dance!

The harbor of New Orleans, at the
mouth of the Mississippi River

Above: a carnival atmosphere prevails
throughout the entire city of New Orleans
during the Mardi Gras. Right: graceful
cypress trees line Louisiana's bayous.

Louisiana's 1,200,000 blacks have suffered from racial prejudice in the past. However, they have made important contributions to American life. Jazz was born in New Orleans' black neighborhoods. Strangely enough, this lively music began at funerals. The mourners would walk in procession to the cemetery, accompanied by a brass band playing sad songs. After the ceremony, the music would take up a fast, African beat. Little by little, in parades, churches, and barbecues, the combination of "brass and beat" caught on. Later, in nightclubs along New Orleans' famous Bourbon Street, great players like Louis "Satchmo" Armstrong and "Jelly Roll" Morton became famous.

AGRICULTURE AND INDUSTRY

A warm, damp climate and the Mississippi's gift of rich soil made Louisiana an agricultural state before the Civil War. Today, only one-fourth of the state's land is used for farming. However, Louisiana ranks among the three leading states in rice production, and second in sugarcane. Cotton, soybeans, sweet potatoes, pecans, and citrus fruits are also grown in Louisiana.

More than half the state is covered with forests, supplying the state's lumber industry. Furs from the state's muskrats, minks, and raccoons, and fish from the Gulf of Mexico are other products of Louisiana.

Another important industry is mining. Louisiana has more oil and natural gas than any other state except Texas. Many of the state's oil wells are located offshore in the Gulf of Mexico. Louisiana also produces 25 percent of the nation's salt and 40 percent of its sulfur, as well as gypsum and limestone.

One of Louisiana's offshore
oil rigs in the Gulf of Mexico

The largest industry in the state is the manufacture of chemicals, particularly those made from oil. Processed food such as sugar, beverages, and baked products also account for much of Louisiana's income.

New Orleans has been a major port since the days of the Louisiana Purchase. A new "superport" called Centroport is now being built along the Mississippi's Gulf outlet. When it is completed in the year 2000 it will ship even more foreign cargo.

ECOLOGY

All of this industry has brought many riches to Louisiana. However, the state's mining and manufacturing have also brought pollution. Oil spills have threatened Louisiana's wildlife, just as they have in Texas. In 1981, the roof of a salt mine under Lake Peigneur collapsed. The lake immediately drained into the mine, taking trees, boats, fish, and two oil rigs with it. Though water from the Gulf of Mexico soon refilled the lake, there was great damage to the area's ecology.

Chemical pollution is another problem. One-fourth of the residents of New Orleans now drink, bathe in, and cook with bottled water because they are worried about chemicals in their tap water. In 1982, a train derailed and spilled a large quantity of poisonous chemicals. Almost 3,000 people had to leave their homes for two weeks to escape the fumes. In the same year, an explosion at a chemical plant caused 20,000 people to flee. Some scientific studies suggest that the state may have a higher than usual cancer rate because of chemical pollution.

CITIES AND SIGHTS

Each year 11,000,000 tourists visit Louisiana. Many stop in New Orleans, one of the prettiest cities in the south central United

New Orleans' picturesque French Quarter

States. Particularly beautiful is a section of the city called the French Quarter. The streets of the French Quarter were laid out by the original French colonists. Much of the architecture reflects New Orleans' Spanish heritage. Many houses are built around patios filled with flowering plants, and most buildings have wrought-iron balconies twisted into lacy shapes. The French Quarter is centuries away from another tourist attraction, the Superdome. Built in 1975, the Superdome is the world's largest enclosed stadium, and the home of the New Orleans Saints football team.

In 1699, a group of French explorers traveling north on the Mississippi saw a tree whose bark had been stripped away and painted red by the Indians to mark a hunting ground boundary. Because of its color, they called it the red staff—*le baton rouge*. Today, Baton Rouge is the capital of Louisiana and the seventh busiest port in the country. The city is also the headquarters of Louisiana's oil and chemical industries.

Shreveport was originally settled by the Caddo Indians. The third largest city in Louisiana, Shreveport is the main recreational and cultural center of the northern part of the state. Many oil and gas companies have offices in Shreveport.

Year admitted to Union: 1812
Capital: Baton Rouge
Nickname: Pelican State
Motto: "Union, Justice, Confidence"
Flower: Indian paintbrush
Bird: brown pelican
Song: "Give Me Louisiana"
Flag: blue with gold border with a pelican
    feeding its young over the
      words "Union, Justice, Confidence."

☆ **6** ☆

ARKANSAS

A famous character in American folklore is the Arkansas Traveler, a well-dressed man making his way through the backwoods of Arkansas. According to the story, the Traveler became lost one day and stopped at a cabin for help. A country fellow was sitting on the porch. "Sir, can you tell me where this road goes?" asked the Traveler. "Well," answered the country fellow, "I've been living here for twenty years and it ain't gone nowhere yet!"

For years, many Americans received a false impression of Arkansas because of the Traveler stories and other tales. They thought all the residents of Arkansas were "hillbillies"—uneducated country folk. This is simply not true, especially now, when half of the state's 2,118,000 people live in modern cities like Little Rock, Fort Smith, and Fayetteville. Today's Arkansan farmers may very well have degrees in agricultural science and use computers to help them figure crop yields and irrigation.

However, there are isolated areas in the state where traditional ways still survive. One of these areas is the Ozark Plateau, in northwestern Arkansas. The first settlers came to the Ozarks in the nineteenth century from Tennesee and Kentucky. They brought musical instruments such as the dulcimer and the auto-

Left: the gently rolling Ozarks.
Above: traditional handicrafts
are a popular attraction at the
Ozark Folk Center.

harp with them, to accompany the ballads they liked to sing. Today, Ozark folk music is very popular, and a yearly festival of music in the Ozark Folk Center is well attended. The Folk Center also displays traditional handicrafts such as quilts, wood carvings, and baskets.

Between the extremes of city and country are small towns, home to many Arkansans. People who live in these towns often praise the peaceful way of life found there. They enjoy the lack of crime, the friendliness of their neighbors, and the clean environment. A country fair always draws a crowd in Arkansas. People work all year to produce a champion—the heaviest watermelon, the most beautiful quilt, the tastiest cherry pie. On fair days, many children have school holidays. They enjoy Ferris wheels and other rides, eat popcorn and chili dogs, and have a wonderful time waiting for the judges' decisions.

About 17 percent of all the people in Arkansas are black. In the past, the state was the scene of some stormy battles for equal rights, such as the one at Little Rock's Central High School in 1957 (see page 23). In recent years, black people have made tremendous progress. Blacks have been elected as mayor and city manager of Little Rock. They have also held responsible positions in the state Senate and the House of Representatives. Many blacks own their own businesses or have good jobs in Arkansas firms. Still, traces of racism remain. In some parts of Arkansas, the rate of unemployment among blacks is twice that of whites. In Little Rock, black income is less than 60 percent of white income. Clearly, more progress must be made before blacks achieve complete equality.

AGRICULTURE AND INDUSTRY

About 40 percent of Arkansas' land is devoted to farming. The state has fertile soil deposits near the Mississippi River, a mild climate, and plenty of rainfall. Arkansas' chief crops include cotton, soybeans, cereal grains, and vegetables. Arkansas also grows more rice than any other state, and raises more broiler chickens. Not surprisingly, the state also produces eggs. Another unusual Arkansas "crop" is catfish. The catfish are raised on "farms" containing huge tanks of water. When they reach marketable size, the fish are shipped to stores and restaurants all over the South.

Over half the state is covered with forests; much of the timber that is harvested is exported to Asia or made into wood and paper products. Other natural resources in Arkansas include gas and oil, and bauxite, a mineral that is made into aluminum. Arkansas produces 96 percent of the nation's bauxite. The state also contains America's only diamond mine. The gems are found in the remains of an ancient volcano near the city of Murfreesboro. The area is now called Crater of Diamonds State Park. Visitors are invited to search for precious stones. Many do, because the rule is "Finders, keepers!"

Throughout most of its history, Arkansas was mainly an agricultural state. After World War II, however, business leaders began to realize that the state deserved its nickname, "the Land of Opportunity." Slowly but surely, new industries have been developed in Arkansas. Winthrop Rockefeller, who was the governor of Arkansas in the late 1960s, persuaded many businesses from other states to establish factories in Arkansas.

Today, manufactured items make up 61 percent of the value of all the goods produced in the state. Processed food such as poultry, soft drinks, and canned goods are produced in Little Rock and Fort Smith. Electronic equipment is also manufactured in Fort Smith, Forrest City, Jacksonville, and other areas. Other important Arkansas industries include the manufacture of metal goods, machinery, and furniture.

In spite of its industrial growth, Arkansas still lags behind much of the United States in per capita income (the amount each person earns). In 1981, Arkansas ranked forty-nine out of the

nation's fifty states. Recently, the state government has been studying ways to bring more industry to Arkansas. One hopeful sign is a $75,000,000 port on the Mississippi River planned for the city of Helena. The project will include a harbor, factories, and a loading terminal, and is expected to create 50,000 new jobs.

CITIES AND SIGHTS

Arkansas' third largest industry is tourism; about 15,000,000 people a year visit the Ozarks, the Ouachita Mountains, and other areas of great natural beauty. The state has almost 3,000,000 acres (1,214,100 ha) of land in national forests and parks, state parks, and wildlife preserves. There is very little pollution in Arkansas, so visitors and residents alike can enjoy clear streams, clean air, and unspoiled forests.

Arkansas' cities also contain many interesting sights. Before the European explorers first arrived in Arkansas, the Indians had two landmarks on opposite sides of the Arkansas River—a big and a little rock. Years later, when settlers founded a city near the second rock, they gave it the obvious name. Today, Little Rock is a bustling, modern city of 160,000, the capital and center of business, education, and culture in Arkansas. Little Rock has several fine museums, including the Arkansas Arts Center and the Museum of Science and History. The Museum of Science and History is located in the Arsenal, a former home for Army officers and their families. The Arsenal is also the birthplace of World War II and Korean War General Douglas MacArthur of the Army. Little Rock has other restored buildings, such as the Terri-

*Cotton is a leading
crop in Arkansas.*

torial Capitol, which dates from 1820, and the Old State House, which is a fine example of traditional southern architecture.

Fort Smith, a major manufacturing center, was a stop for travelers to the West during the Gold Rush of 1849. The city was once a wild frontier town, but was brought to law and order by Isaac Parker, the "Hanging Judge." The Judge got his name from the eighty-three men he sent to the gallows between 1875 and 1896. Fort Smith is now the second largest city in Arkansas, and is the site of more than 200 factories.

Year admitted to Union: 1836
Capital: Little Rock
Nickname: Land of Opportunity
Motto: *"Regnat Populus"* ("The People Rule")
Flower: Apple blossom
Bird: mockingbird
Song: "Arkansas"
Flag: red with a large white diamond in the
      center. In the diamond are four stars and
      the word "Arkansas." The diamond
      has a blue border lined with stars.

*Competition between
college football teams
in the south central states
is intense. Here it's "The
Annual Shoot-out" between
the Arkansas Razorbacks
and the Texas Longhorns.*

CONCLUSION

As we approach the year 2000, the south central states face many challenges. Sometime during the next century (no one knows exactly when) the rich oil deposits of the area will run dry. The states are planning for that day by seeking other types of industries. Computer products and other advanced technology will be especially important. Some cities in the south central states are also trying to increase their foreign trade, selling themselves as "the gateway to South America" and establishing "free trade" zones, where foreign businesses receive tax breaks.

The south central states are also dealing with the problems caused by their tremendous growth, such as crime and pollution. In some places, the south central states are also coping with racial tensions, trying to insure that minority groups share equally in the wealth of the land. The outcome of these struggles will determine the quality of life in the south central states for years to come.

INDEX

Adobe houses, 25
Aerospace industry, 34
Agriculture and industries.
 See industries and agriculture
Alamo, 11, 12
Aliens, illegal, 27
Angora goats, 27
Animals, 2, 3
"Annual Shoot-out" (football), 60
Apache tribe, 5, 16
Arkansas, 53–61
Arkansas Arts Center, 59
Arkansas Post, 9
Arkansas Traveler, 53
"Arkies," 20
Armadillo, 3
Armstrong, Louis, 49
Arsenal, 59
Astrodome, 32
Attacapa tribe, 5
Austin, 32
Autoharp 53, 56

Baton Rouge, 52
Battle of San Jacinto, 12
 monument, 32

Bauxite mining, 57
Bayous, 2
Bienville, Jean Baptiste, 9
"Black gold," 43
"Blow-outs," 31
Blue Northers, 3
Bonaparte, Napoleon, 10
"Boomers," 16
Boucherie, 45
Bourbon Street, 49
Bowie, Jim, 12
"Brass and beat," 49
Bryan, John Neely, 34

Caddo tribe, 5
Cajuns, 45
Catfish farms, 57
Cattle, 17, 26, 32
 roundup, 26
 Texas, 27
Central Plains, 3
Centroport, 50
Chemical production, 50
Cherokee tribe, 13
Cheyenne tribe, 5
Chickasaw tribe, 13

Choctaw tribe, 13
Cisneros, Henry, 27
Civil rights struggle, 23
Civil War, 13, 15–16
Climate, 2–3
Comanche tribe, 16
Computer industry, 34
Confederate States of America, 15
Coronado, Francisco, 6
Cotton growing, 27, 38, 58
Covered wagons, 16
Cowboys, 25
    Hall of Fame, 42
"Cow town," 41
Crater of Diamonds State Park, 57
Creek tribe, 13
Creoles, 44
Crockett, Davy, 11, 12

Dallas, 34
"Deep South," 1
Delta, 4
Depression, 20
DeSoto, Hernando, 6
DeTonti, Henri, 9
DeVaca, Cabeza, 6
Diamond mine, 57
Discrimination, 20, 22, 23, 25, 27, 37
    Arkansas, 56
    Louisiana, 49
Dulcimer, 53
Dust Bowl, 20, 37

Economic boom in Texas, 28
Economic growth, effect of, 31
Employment
    Arkansas, 56, 59
    Oklahoma, 37, 41
    Texas, 28, 31

Environmentalists
    Louisiana, 50
    Oklahoma, 41
    Texas, 31–32
Equality, struggle for, 20, 23
European settlement, 6, 8

Fair Park, 34
Fais dodo, 45
"Fat Tuesday," 45
"Five Civilized Tribes," 13
Football, 32, 52
Fort Smith, 53, 61
French and Indian War, 9
French Canadians, 45
French Quarter, New Orleans, 51, 52

Geography, 1–4
Goat raising, 27
Gold Rush, 61
Great Depression, 20
Great Plains, 3
"GTT," 12
Gulf Coastal Plain, 2
Gulf of Mexico, 4, 10, 32

"Hanging judge," 61
Higgins, Pattillo, 19
"Hillbillies," 53
History of the area, 23
Homesteaders, 35
Houston, 30, 32, 33
Houston Ship Channel, 32, 33

Illegal aliens, 27
Indians, 9. See also individual tribes
    in Arkansas, 59
    in Oklahoma, 35, 37
Indian City, 37
Indian dance festivals, 36

Indian Territory, 13, 16, 19, 35
Industries
    aerospace, 34
    computer, 34
Industries and agriculture
    Arkansas, 56–57, 59
    Louisiana, 49–50
    Oklahoma, 37–38, 41
    Texas, 27–28

Jazz, birthplace of, 49
Jefferson, Thomas, 9–10
Johnson Library, 32
Joliet, Louis, 6

Karankawa tribe, 5
King Ranch, 27

Lake Peigneur, 50
"Land of Opportunity," 57
Land Rush, 16, 19, 35
LaSalle, Robert, 6
Law, John, 43
Little Rock, Arkansas, 23, 56, 59
Livestock in Oklahoma, 37
Lone Star State, 24
Louisiana, 43–52
Louisiana Purchase, 8, 9–10
Louisiana Territory, 9
Lumber, 49

MacArthur, Douglas, 59
Manufacturing, in Texas, 28
Mardi Gras, 45, 46
Marquette, Jacques, 6
Meat-packing, 41
Mexican aliens, 27
Mexican-Americans, 25, 27
Mexican Highlands, 3
Mexico, Republic of, 10
Mining, 49

Mission, Spanish, 9
Mississippi Delta, 4
Mississippi River, 3–4, 6, 42
Morton, "Jelly Roll," 49
Mung beans production, 38
Murfreesboro, 57
Museum of Science and History, 59
Music, Ozark, 55–56

Napolean Bonaparte, 10
NASA's Mission Control, 25
National Cowboy Hall of Fame, 42
New Orleans, 9, 43, 44, 50, 51, 52
North Central Plains, 3

Ogallala Formation, 32
Oil, 19–20
    formation of, 1–2
    Louisiana, 48, 49
    Oklahoma, 38, 39
    Texas, 28, 32
"Oil Capital of the World," 42
"Okies," 20
Oklahoma, 13, 17, 19, 20, 35–42
Oklahoma City, 35, 41–42
Old State House, 61
Osage tribe, 5
Ouachita Mountains, 3, 59
Ozark Folk Center, 55, 56
Ozark Plateau, 2, 53
Ozarks, 54, 55, 59
    music, 56

Parker, Judge Isaac, 61
Pawnee tribe, 16
Pecan growing, 38
Plantation system, 15
Prehistoric societies, 5

Quapaw tribe, 5

Ranches, Texas, 27
Recession, 28
Republic of Mexico, 10
Republic of Texas, 12
Rice growing, 49, 57
Rio del Espiritu Santo, 6
Rivers, 4
"River of the Holy Spirit," 6
Rockefeller, Winthrop, 57
Roosevelt, Franklin D., 20

Salt production, 49
San Jacinto, 12, 32
Schools, early, 17
Seminole tribe, 13
Sheep raising, 27
Shell Oil, 29
Shreveport, 52
Shrimp production, 27
Slavery, 15, 20
"Sooner State," 35
Sorghum grain production, 27
Spanish heritage, 52
Spindletop, Texas, 19
Spindletop oil strike, 18

State Historical Museum, 42
Sugarcane, 49
Sun Belt, 1
Superdome, 52

Temperatures, 2
Terrain, 2
Territorial Capital, 61
Texas, 10, 24–34
"Tex-Mex," 25
Thornton, R. L., 1
Timber, 57
Tonkawa tribe, 5
"Trail of Tears," 13, 14
Travis, William, 12
Tribes. Indian, 13. See also individu-
   al tribes
Tulsa, 42

Unemployment, 20

Weather, 2
Winter wheat, 38
Wool production, 27
World War II, 20

XIT Ranch, 24, 27